FANTASTIC SPORTS FACTS

RACING

Michael Hurley

Chicago, Illinois

Edited by Catherine Veitch, Sian Smith,
   and John-Paul Wilkins
Designed by Richard Parker
Picture research by Ruth Blair
Originated by Capstone Global Library Ltd
Printed and bound in China

16 15 14 13 12
10 9 8 7 6 5 4 3 2 1

Library of Congress Cataloging-in-Publication Data
Cataloging-in-Publication data is available at the Library
of Congress.
ISBN 978-1-4109-5105-2 (hbk)
ISBN 978-1-4109-5112-0 (pbk)

Acknowledgments
We would like to thank the following for permission to
reproduce photographs: Corbis pp. 7 (© Leo Mason), 9 (©
Schlegelmilch), 12 (© Clifford White), 16 (© Rainer Ehrhardt/
ZUMA Press), 18 (© George Tiedemann), 24 (© PCN), 25 (©
Melchert Harry/dpa), 27 (© Robert Sullivan /Reuters); Getty
Images p. 5 (Karl Johaentges); Photoshot pp. 6 (© Icon SMI),
10 (© Imagebrokers), 11 (© UPPA), 19 (© Talking Sport),
20, 21, 23 (© Picture Alliance), 26 (© Everett Collection);
© Photoshot p. 17; Shutterstock pp. 4 (© Natursports), 8 (©
AHMAD FAIZAL YAHYA), 11 (© Richard Peterson), 13
kangaroo (© Eric Isselée), 13 stop sign (© Luca Villanova), 14
(© cjmac), 15 (© CHEN WS), 21 (© Nataliia Natykach), 22 (©
Studio 1a Photography).

Cover photograph of Sebastian Vettel reproduced with
permission of Corbis (© SRDJAN SUKI/epa), and a car wheel
reproduced with permission of Shutterstock (© risteski goce).

Every effort has been made to contact copyright holders
of any material reproduced in this book. Any omissions
will be rectified in subsequent printings if notice is given
to the publisher.

Contents

Some words are printed in bold, **like this**. You can find out what they mean by looking in the glossary.

Motor Sports Basics

Motor sports are very popular all over the world. They are exciting, fast, and dangerous.

The Nurburgring racetrack in Germany was opened in 1927. It is one of the longest in the world.

The Fastest

The fastest vehicles used in motor sports are **drag racing** cars. They have a top speed of 330 miles per hour (531 kilometers per hour).

DID YOU KNOW?

The fastest motorcycles are also drag racers. They have a top speed of 245 miles per hour (395 kilometers per hour).

Getting Ahead

In motor sports, gaining an edge over others can mean the difference between winning and losing.

The huge rear wing on this car helps to keep it steady at high speeds.

rear wing

extra wheel

DID YOU KNOW?

In the 1970s, **Tyrrell** developed a racer with six wheels. This amazing car won the 1976 Swedish Grand Prix.

Unusual Racers

If a vehicle has an engine, you can race it! One of the most exciting motor sports is truck racing.

DID YOU KNOW?

Racing trucks have to weigh at least 12,000 pounds—the same as a male elephant!

You can race lawn mowers, too! Racers improve their mowers so that they **accelerate** more quickly.

WHAT WILL PEOPLE BE RACING NEXT?!

Kangaroo Stops Race!

In 2007, during the famous Bathurst 1000 race in Australia, a kangaroo appeared and bounced around on the racetrack! Incredibly, no one was injured, and the kangaroo escaped unhurt.

13

Pit Crews

Pit crews help make their team's vehicle work properly. During a pit stop, the pit crew has to work as a team to replace the tires. A good pit crew can help a team win a race.

DID YOU KNOW?

In **Formula 1**, all four tires can be changed in less than three seconds!

24-Hour Racing

The famous Le Mans 24-Hour race takes place in Le Mans, France. Each car has a team of drivers who take over for each other during the race. They race through the night.

DID YOU KNOW?

At the 2011 race, British driver Allan McNish crashed his race car at almost 140 miles per hour (225 kilometers per hour). He was lucky to be unharmed.

Giant Crowds

The Indianapolis 500 takes place every year at the Indianapolis Motor Speedway in Indiana. More than 400,000 people turn up to watch this race!

The Daytona 500 race attracts over 180,000 **spectators**.

DID YOU KNOW?

The Indianapolis Motor Speedway is also known as the "Brickyard." The racetrack was originally built out of bricks!

The Race of Champions

The drivers compete in different vehicles to see who is the best.

At the end of every year, there is a spectacular event for all the world's best drivers. The Race of Champions takes place inside a sports stadium.

Sebastien Ogier won the Race of Champions on his first attempt.

DID YOU KNOW?

French racing star Sebastien Ogier won the 2011 Race of Champions.

Highest-Paid Driver

The best drivers and riders in the world are very well-paid. Two-time **Formula 1** world champion Fernando Alonso, who drives for Ferrari, is paid an incredible $36 million a year!

The steering wheel on a Formula 1 car costs about $30,000. That is more than most normal cars cost!

Great Drivers

Sebastian Vettel won the **Formula 1** World Championship in 2010 and 2011. Vettel is the youngest driver ever to win a world championship. He started by racing **go-karts** when he was just seven years old.

RECORD BREAKERS

Michael Schumacher won a record 91 races in his Formula 1 career.

American driver Danica Patrick is the most successful female racer in the world. She started racing **go-karts** at 10 years of age.

In 2008, Patrick became the first woman to win an **IndyCar** race.

RECORD BREAKERS

Legendary driver Jimmie Johnson won the **NASCAR** Sprint Cup Series championship five times in a row, which is an amazing record in the sport.

Quiz

Are you a superfan or a couch potato? Decide whether the statements below are true or false. Then look at the answers on page 31 and check your score on the fanometer.

1 Finnish driver Kimi Raikkonen has driven in **Formula 1, World Rally,** and **NASCAR.**

2 The fastest Formula 1 **pit crews** can change all four wheels in five seconds.

3 Lewis Hamilton is the youngest ever Formula 1 world champion.

4 Jimmie Johnson has won four NASCAR Sprint Cup Series championships.

5 Ferrari has won more Formula 1 races than any other team.

6 The top speed of a **drag racing** motorcycle is 186 miles (300 kilometers) per hour.

FANOMETER

fair-weather fan

couch potato

superfan

1 2 3 4 5 6

Glossary

accelerate speed up

drag racing timed race over a short distance, usually a quarter of a mile

Formula 1 type of racing series. Formula 1 cars have an open cockpit and uncovered wheels.

go-kart small, four-wheeled vehicle used in racing

IndyCar type of racing series. IndyCar cars have an open cockpit and uncovered wheels.

MotoGP type of racing series. This is the motorcycle version of Formula 1.

NASCAR type of racing series. NASCAR cars are like normal road cars, but much faster.

pit crews group of people who work as a team to make sure that a car is ready to race

pit stop when a car comes into the pits to have the tires changed by the pit crew

spectators group of people who watch a game or show

Tyrrell Formula 1 team in the 1970s

World Rally also known as the World Rally Championship (WRC), this is a racing series. These cars do not race on racetracks, but rather on public roads in timed stages.

Find Out More

Books

Gifford, Clive. *The Inside Story of Motorsports* (Sports World). New York: Rosen, 2012.

Kelley, K. C. *NASCAR* (Racing Mania). New York: Marshall Cavendish Benchmark, 2010.

Websites

Facthound offers a safe, fun way to find Internet sites related to this book. All of the sites on Facthound have been researched by our staff.

Here's all you do:

Visit www.facthound.com

Type in this code: 9781410951052

Quiz answers

1) True.
2) False. It only takes the top teams about three seconds to change all four wheels (see page 15)!
3) False. Sebastian Vettel became the youngest ever Formula 1 world champion in 2010 (see page 24).
4) False. Johnson has won five NASCAR championships (see page 27).
5) True.
6) False. These motorcycles can go faster than 245 miles per hour (395 kilometers per hour) (see page 7)!

Index